MW00413453

BENEATH
a
WILLOW
TREE

Poems by LUCY WYER

Light Dancing on Water LLC
Bend, Oregon

Light Dancing on Water LLC
Bend, Oregon
www.lucywyer.com

Copyright 2021 Lucy Wyer

Book Design: Bright Light Graphics, LLC
Cover photo: Joseph Gonzalez
Author photo: Richard Breitung

ISBN 978-1-7362793-0-4 Paperback
ISBN 978-1-7362793-1-1 eBook
ISBN 978-1-7362793-2-8 Audiobook available with original music

Library of Congress Control Number: 2020925526

I bless the Mighty Winds that blow
all these extraordinary beings
and exquisite storms into my life
so that I may be here, now, with you.

you are amazing!

Love,

Lucy

TABLE OF CONTENTS

I. SPRING

May these poems playfully serve you
in falling utterly in love with your life
amid the truth of Nature's benevolent wisdom.

Beneath a Willow Tree

[I]

SPRING

APHRODITE'S DOVE

Last night the Moon
crawled into my bed.
We made love in stillness.
Ravished by madness,
I rolled over and slept heavy
under its fullness.
Sometime before dawn
I dreamt my heart burst open
and out flew Aphrodite's dove.
This morning I am pregnant
with the moon's Presence.
Ready to give birth
to new possibility.

MAKING SWEET HONEY

Like a bee, seek nectar everywhere.
Fall deep into the alchemy of flower and sunlight,
where pollen and procreation unite.
Enticed by each flower's essence,
be curious—what's in there, magic or mayhem?
Go ahead, dive in anyway,
fall drunk on the nectar.
Your life will become juicy.

Like a flower, become your own unique expression.
Give more nectar than you can possibly give,
then give some more.
Make offerings everywhere you go,
enjoying the fruits of your allurement.

The bee takes great pleasure in gathering pollen.
The flower yields with exquisite delight.
The sun blazing equally on them both.
Bee humming happily making sweet honey,
flower in delicate repose,
each euphoric in this whirling romance.

Like bee and flower,
wander free among the meadow,
in a dance of divine rhythm and love.
Intoxicated with nectar, go wherever you please,
making sweet honey.
So free every act of expression is rebellion.
What then will be born of your inner sunlight?

TWO RIVERS

Lover, hear my longing.
I am she who is the confluence
of two deep rivers.

One, sourced from my knowing
that every moment is indeed sacred,
in service to the vast Oneness that holds me.
This is the pure spring that feeds my joy,
the source of my unabating freedom.

The other river my contentment,
my love of the unknown.
No need to know where
these waters will take me.
I have deep faith in the winds
and currents
that carried me here
to this convergence.

I am the source and the river itself,
a blending of waters
merging erotic creative energies
with the sacred,
bringing my gifts to the world.
The sound of my voice wants to run
clear and free,
wild and flowing.
These waters have no need
to contain their intensity.

A web of wisdom hangs low over the water—
catching drops that spray from the love
that manifests through my boldness.
I stand proudly in this precious moment
even as I waver with the force
calling me forward,
for I know I must move on.

I am she who is willing to drown for love.
She who knows the waters will carry her,
support her, enliven her, delight her, heal her.
She who knows intimately that these waters
make love to her with a powerful rushing force.

I know you are afraid of my intensity,
for if you lie down with me,
you might drown in the potency of our union.
Take my hand and surrender to my flow.
A natural buoyancy,
born of our unwillingness
to be held down for any reason,
will keep our heads and hearts high.

Relax in my waters,
in deep knowing that I carry you,
for you can not be held down
when we are joined together in splendor.
Let us meander together as lovers
joined in sacred union
at the confluence of two deep rivers.

FALLING IN LOVE

It's easy to fall in love with Nature.
Nature always returns the embrace.
Provides us with nourishment, beauty,
sunshine and starlight.

Inspires us to dance
through the cycles and seasons,
of life.

Flows our waters
through contraction
and expansion
in rhythm with the moon.

Guides us deeper
into faith
as we weather
every storm.

Yes, it is easy to fall in love with Nature.
Nature always returns the embrace.

Can we fall in love with ourselves,
possibly even all of life,
with the same potency?
For we too are a miracle
of Nature.

LOVE POEMS

What happened
to all the love poems
I wrote,
tore up in tiny pieces,
and threw away?

Sent floating down the river
in my desperate bargaining
that the price
was too high
to send them
out into the world.

They came back
in the spring
as rain.

MIGHTY WINDS

Go where the mighty winds take you,
dressed only in the cloak of immediacy.

Rocky outcrops will not harm you,
mountain columbine will fragrance you,
eagle feathers will soften you,
wayward peaks will inspire you.

When you leap you will not fall,
as you soar you will have wings,
in your flight you will know insight.

Go where the mighty winds take you,
dressed only in the cloak of immediacy.

You will move beyond
the bounds of time,
where we wake
from this bewildering dream.

BUSHWHACK

I used to bushwhack
my way through life
like a bear just up
from winter's rest—
intent on finding
the most luscious berries
in random places.

Now I'm more berry
than bear.

CONSIDER YOUR SOURCE

Is love flowing from you as intensely
as a mountain stream in springtime?

Maybe it's time to reconsider your Source.

Do you believe the natural world
loves you as much as you love Nature?

Maybe you can start there.

Only the potency that never pauses
will flow over the debris
in your water.

You were born to flow freely
toward the ocean,
merge in communion
with all that is sacred.

Does every rain bath, every bird song,
every sun melt add to your flow?

Maybe now is the time
to consider your Source.

[II]

SUMMER

WILD FREEDOM

I am the face of wild freedom.
The radiance of earth,
the mystery of fire,
the healing force of water,
the power of air.

I am the alluring magic
of the Moon and the Sun
dancing with the planets
as they delight in the Stars.

I am the innocence at the heart of life,
the consciousness that enlivens,
brings life to all beings,
all of creation—through love.

I am this spacious, ethereal moment
in the pendulum of existence.
From me all is born,
and will eventually return—
to my soils, to my waters, to my depth.

I am the wind that blows seeds in all directions,
propagating beauty in the heart of existence.
I am the roots that take pleasure in the earth.
My water nourishes every morsel of life.
I am the fires of transformation—
encouraging life to evolve, to thrive, to flourish.

I am the creative force of allurement.
I attract the bees to the flowers,
the tides to the Moon,
the male to the female.

I am the energy that rejoices in well being
for that is my true nature.
There is no need to strive for me,
or search for me,
for I am already you,
you are already me.

TOO

I have fallen in love
with a river.
The river makes love
to me too.
Together we long
for the ocean.
The ocean longs
for us too.

FOREST ALLIANCE

If you come upon me
dancing
in a forest clearing
do not be afraid.

I am not astray.
I am dancing to the rhythm
of the sublime.

The trees and I are in alliance
creating an entire new world
born of our harmony.

They circle around me
I dance for them.
We all take great pleasure.

Do not be shy,
even if you can not yet
hear our music.

Join us.
How we step on the earth
creates the world we desire.

WILD MUSTANG

The wild mustang I corralled broke free.
I could mend the fence,
or just chase after him.
Either way I am still tethered.

What if I did nothing.
Just let him return,
to live by my side
with no gate to hold him.

Kept my heart open
amid the never ending
possibility
of his departure.

I was drawn by his wild untamable nature.
I wanted to make it mine.

I know the real truth is to set myself free.
Gallop across arid desert plains and head for the mountains.
Fly at neck-breaking speed with rays of golden light streaming.
Use only my old broke heart to guide me.

Maybe then I will live
with the wild freedom
that is calling me.

Maybe then I will finally catch up
with the winds
that can carry me home.

STELLAR'S JAY

I met a magician on my hike today
scrambling up a mountain trail.

Paused to catch my breath—
lost love momentarily forgotten.

He danced around me three times
before he flew to a nearby branch
to sing me a love song.

Preened his blue feathers as if
for my pleasure alone.
What a flirt!

Reeling me in
he cast his spell.
I can love again.

Not I but the winds carry my children into the world.
I watch from distant branch,
singing love songs of encouragement.
Look at them with eyes of love
so they can see their own beauty.
Watch over them with tenderness
as their subtle, delicate wings take flight.
Know their gifts of creativity and sensitivity
might wound them as they learn to fly.
I'm not an easy mother to have.

Not I but the winds inspire them to take flight.
I give them freedom—yet not tell them to how to fly.
I sit in my branch with compassionate knowing
that they too have to find their own wings.
They want to be free, so they jump.
I'm not an easy mother to have.

I keep singing my love songs of encouragement.
Look at them with the eyes of love
so they discover their own beauty.
I keep finding my own way to fly.

Not I but the winds blow fierce love through their bones.
I am parent witness to offspring
harnessing their own wind to take flight.
Watch as they fall forcibly on the ground,
pick themselves up,
then look around for what to do next.
I have already flown off.
I'm not an easy mother to have.

Not I but the winds create their beauty,
teach them to sing their own love songs,
watch with softhearted acceptance and empathy
as they are challenged by the chaos that courses through life.
I am learning to harness my own winds,
navigate my own storms.
I'm not an easy mother to have.

I sing my love songs of encouragement.
Look at them with the eyes of love
so they discover their own beauty.
I fly away and tell them to have fun,
tell them everything will work out.
I trust in Nature's wisdom to guide us all.

None of my children have roosted near by.
We each flew far away and made our own nests.
I honor this paradox—
still sing my love songs for them,
which call to the winds that feather our souls.

All Nature's children are creative.
All Nature's children are beautiful.
All Nature's children know how to fly in freedom.

MOONLIT LAKE

Do not be so loyal to your thoughts.
They are only informative undulations on your lake.
Slip naked into tranquil waters—beneath a moonlit night.
Quiet into the depths of your own being.
An atmosphere of purity will engulf you.

Imagine floating with only the night sky sustaining you.

Be the lake that reflects the moon and sparkles in stillness,
a reflective pool through which consciousness becomes aware.
Nothing is more luminous than the space
with which the world arises and subsides.

Imagine what might happen if you suddenly dove
beneath the turbulence on the surface
and came up in freedom.

Enriched by the magic of the moon,
stars will write you messages of navigation,
stir your imagination into the visionary realms.
A deep reverence for eternal and ancient mysteries
will encompass your inner space.

Imagine what beauty could be created from your being.

Do not be so loyal to your thoughts.
They are only gentle undulations on your lake.
Luxuriate in silence as your purest expression.
You will become so radiant
the fish will long to see your face.

RIVER TRAIL

I wish I'd taken
the river trail
even though
it was muddy
and even
a little slippery.

Then I would not
have disturbed
all the butterflies
sunbathing
on the fire road.

[III]

FALL

CLOUDS

I'd like to write a poem about clouds.
How they usher in a new world
with each passing storm.

Drawing me in
and out again
like magic.
Congregate
or dissipate
faithfully
at exactly
the perfect moment
to mirror my mood.

Yes, I'd like to write a poem
about clouds.
But they are just too lovely
and ethereal
to put into words.

SECRETS

If you are afraid
for the future of this earth
and all its glorious creatures,
take refuge
in an old-growth
forest thicket.

Go with gratitude
and an openness
to discover
new possibility.

Step tenderly,
and lovingly
to where
diverse roots
intertwine.

There you will recognize
the trees are breathing
and swaying
your name.

Join in their
dance
of optimistic
decay.

The miraculous
fungal network
beneath your feet
will not be lost
on you.

Sink deeply into
the wisdom of this
mycelial mosaic.

The forest will hold you
with such endearment
they will gladly reveal
all their secrets to you.

BENEATH A WILLOW TREE

Asleep beneath a willow tree,
I wake in watery grave.
In casket woven from willow's arms,
embraced in fluid grace.

Moonlight far above me
reflects in surface waves,
dances down to greet me
with loving lucid gaze.

My past a corpse beneath me,
destiny unknown,
I lie in comfort knowing
that mystery is my home.

I wonder of this spark of life,
forged in fluid flesh,
that draws my breath
and swaddles me
with golden timelessness.

Translucent now,
I see my strength
in vulnerability lay.

"Rise up, dear one,"
the waters call
"to take this gift away."

I find upon my fingers touch,
an arrow made of light,
and in my hands a bow is drawn,
to hold alongside my heart.

I am no more the body
that carried me to sleep.
Propelled to water's surface,
I emerge with swiftness deep.

At one with bow and arrow,
my target still unknown,
I trust my aim and focus,
for eternity is now my home.

BED OF MOSS

Quiet your lonely heart.
Stretch out your arms,
circle around a forest floor.

Ask to enter its mystery,
seek to know its magic.
An opening will rise up
and embrace you.
Your beautiful companions
will find you.

Pause. Listen. Breathe.
The forest, a living, breathing, sacred entity,
alive with life—
speaks to you.
A deep-rooted harmony
will reveal itself.

Ask permission to know
them intimately.
Witness the completeness,
the peacefulness,
the wholeness of it all.

Bow in devotion.
Regard the forest
with deep reverence.
Feel the loving arms
of community all around.

Talk eagerly of love to each tree,
each bush, each dancing bird.
Speak openly of your longing.
Prayers set to wind flutter joy in dappled light.

Lay back and relax.
Allow the soft bed of moss to rise up,
comfort you.
Let them do what they do best.

Recognize your own beauty
in every radiant expression of life.
Awaken to communion with the forest.
Your heart will rise up
whispering love songs
of endless astonishment and delight.

TENDER PARTS

Fierce winds
tried to rip
all my clothes off
as I walked across
a fertile prairie.

I suppose
I was walking
so softly,
caressing the
grasses with
my bare feet,
gently trying not to harm
any tender parts,
that they wanted
some loving too.

Next time
I will try
and remember
to leave nothing out
of my heart.

THE BEAUTY YOU ARE

Do you have any idea how exquisite you are?
I think not my dear.
Let Nature's beauty show you.

For you are as magical as the wonder
of the night sky, the radiance of a full moon,
the mystery that lies at the heart of a roaring fire.

You are as extraordinary as the sound
of rushing water madly cascading over rock in a stream.
As magnificent as anything in the natural world
for you were made from stardust,
atoms at play for billions of years.
Earth, air, water, fire—the same energy
and intelligence that created all of life.

Nature inspires you to see beauty,
but you create the enchantment.
Draw breath in the presence of splendor—
tap into the timelessness of existence.

That moment resonates so deeply
with your essential nature
that the beauty you observe—
reflects the beauty you are.

You recognize the peace and beauty
inherent in Nature
because you are that peace and beauty—
you are Nature itself.

HEY BABE

I used to wonder
what to call
the divine energy
I saw in every
tree, bird
trout,
and rainbow.

And what I felt about
that moon
made me blush.

So instead, I began
to bow
to every mountain,
chipmunk
and river curve
that caught my eye.

But all that
bending over
got much too taxing.

I kept tripping
over rocks
and missing
other earthly delights.

These days I just say
"Hey Babe!"
to everything I behold
in the natural world.

Now I am much
more intimate
with all I perceive.

FOREST OF GOLD

If you are fortunate enough
to wander
into a Larch grove
in late autumn,
after the Aspen leaves
have done their dance,
move silently, with reverence.
If the winds are kind,
you might be blessed
by grace.

Ethereal Larch needles
subtly rain down
all around you
in luminous golden swirls
before falling
on the forest floor
with gracious elegance.

Imagine being the only conifer tree
in a field of pines
that loses its needles every fall.

Can you be that lovely
exposed to the elements?
Can you be that willing
to illuminate
all that is around you
even as you let go
of memories you cherish?

[IV]
WINTER

WINTER'S CALLING

You might not see me for a while.
A blanket of darkness is drawing me inward.
Do not despair for me—I am not lost.
The Moon knows where I am.
The Stars still ask to dance.

If you join me, I will fiercely guard your solitude.
We can dance inspired by the dark night sky,
play among the constellations,
shape-shift to suit our moods.

The darkness will be my arms holding you tight.
As I tumble through the deepening sky,
rolling with the ecstasy of divine mystery,
you will be making your own sweet love with wonder.

Our dance will be as two star struck lovers
coming together only in Spirit.
The Moon can be our secret place
to rendezvous for one brief kiss
before we playfully bow to each other
and float away, laughing.

The dark womb is my bedroom tonight.
It holds me in tender embrace as I shed my tears.
Do not despair for me when I wander in darkness.
I am not lost.
I am dancing though the night sky
in a waltz with wonder and magic.

HAWK EYES

I was a hawk circling
my own innocence.

Set my sights on the most
vicious place to lacerate.
Came up victorious,
and bloody.

Everything that was missing
funneled into that wound.
An unstoppable portal of pain.

Years later I fell to my knees
and cried for forgiveness.

The hawk circled again.

This time with eyes of wisdom
to pick me up and carry me off
into profound freedom.

Our wounds call us to love's door.
Walk proudly through.
Do not accept anything less
than the medicine of radical forgiveness.

LOVE CHILD

This morning I gave birth
to a new possibility.

What if everything born
in this world is
a love child?
Hummingbird, blade of grass,
infant child, newborn elephant.

Whatever creates the conception—
a rape, a ravishment,
a longing, a light.
Something beautiful
is always born.

Beyond judgement,
we learn to love
what is emerging
from the dark womb.

For when love is born
of our acceptance,
our heart breaks open
with whatever
causes innocence
to cry out
in the night.

SHOOTING STAR

I was a shooting star
tumbling through the night sky
circling the planets
searching for a tender embryo.

I was willing to land
just long enough to dance
new love into a dark womb.

I was a shooting star
tumbling through the night sky
circling the planets
searching for a gentle soul,
one with a heart that is tear-shaped,
so she could feel more deeply.

I knew this one would go all in—
dive into love wholeheartedly.
We'd get our heart broken
over and over again.
And it would open us.

I was a shooting star
tumbling through the night sky
circling the planets
searching for a sensitive being
strong enough to hold onto
her joyful innocence.

I found gold.

SACRED SEEDS

Oh Sacred One,
What seeds did you plant in my soil?
Why do I feel such intense desire,
such longing to be completely swept over?

Did you secretly know I was fertile?
You knelt down beside me.
Stared at me with those eyes.
Left me ripe and vulnerable.

I opened just enough
for you to slip into my soft folds.

Now the ground is hardened.
I will have to wait for the rains to soften.
Why do you torment me with such lust for spring?

Oh Sacred One, if this is your way
of teasing me into fullness,
I surrender.

EAGLE'S WATCH

I wake to news
of destruction,
devastation—
oh my beloved planet.

Despair splits a fissure
through my heart.

I want to hide,
never again associate
with injustice beyond
my comprehension.

I strap on my
hiking boots
anyway,
and step outside
to paint a new dawn.

Turning toward a pond,
I startle a bald eagle
gathering grasses.

I pause on the shoreline,
he lands in a tree.

I weep in gratitude
for his attention
and ask,
how can I fight
when I only want
to love?

My heart hears his answer:

Beyond envy, greed or fear
lies a strength within you.
Give without need
of anything in return.

Summon the courage
to write another love poem
to Nature.

That is enough.

THIRTEENTH MOON

A thirteenth Full Moon slips in every winter
just before the earth's orbit around the sun
to remind us of the beauty of darkness
turning to light.

How curious so many of us prefer
light over dark, summer over winter.
We are drawn to the light for that is our true nature,
yet darkness is an essential element in our
recognition of luminosity within.

The beauty of winter is conducive to making love
with the dark.

We are most grateful after cold evenings draw us together
to comfort, to nourish, to care
for each other with quiet contentment.

Long nights in the shadows
just before the mystique of sleep sets in
encourage us to make love to our dreams,
whether they lie next to us,
or remain on the horizon.

Stretches of inner wilderness insulate us
from distraction and disturbance,
serve the incubation of what is emerging,
awakening the waves of inspiration and change.

For only in a dark womb are the most vast
treasures of life revealed,
through the sweet mystery
inherent in the unknown.

It takes great love and courage
to surrender to loving darkness so much
it becomes its own unique light.
To love what wants to be born
from the shadows.

Light or dark, I am not sure which side I choose.
It hardly matters anyway.
They are equally beautiful
to my soul.

Winter holds the profound peacefulness
that exists when my mind relaxes in
embrace with my heart.
Summer holds the ecstasy of energy
dancing through me as I delight
in Nature's grace.

Neither is right or wrong, good or bad,
I am going to experience both no matter what,
but I do know I prefer to make love
over any other way of being.

Give me a Full Moon over fallen snow
and I am drawn into the magical slowing of time
through the beauty, serenity, tranquility
of moonlight upon powdery snow.

I move into the quickening radiance of spring,
more ready to honor the unrecognizable
after a winter that drew me inward
unafraid to dance one more time
with the Moon.

As I awaken after heartfelt darkness
to linger in dawn's light
making love—
I discover the
exquisiteness of quietude.

CLIMB NAKED

The man I love
is hiding
in a cave
on the mountain.

So every night
I climb naked
up the snowy peaks
following his tracks
which have long
since vanished.

Some day
he will peak
his head out
and laugh
at my audacity.

Spring will arrive.

[V]

FOR ALL SEASONS

AN EMERGING PROMISE

Rise before dawn and lift the veil from your weary heart—
make a promise you have no desire but to keep.
Open your inner gaze to the knowing
that your dreams kiss you on the forehead, and say:
wake up my dear, now is your time.
Whisper your devotion to the new world
that arrives each day,
cleansed and renewed,
ready to make your life lovely and whole.

There is a deep release in your sublime recognition
that every single moment in your life
brought you here, to this one dreamy kiss.
You are a bud at the center of a self
that wants to flower into fullness with all of life.

Build yourself a new home,
born from the lingering memory of that embrace,
one with an expansive view that stretches
far beyond your wildest imagination.
Create a sanctuary of all that you love,
all that you hold most dear,
then stand in wonder and awe of your good fortune.

Let your heart wander lonely into dense woods
at night in need of intimacy.
Surrender to the love that surrounds you
in the shadows.
Love the darkness of the unknown
so completely that it turns to dawn's light.
That alone will set you free.

Make fresh tracks in powdery snow beneath a full moon.
Stop to lie down beneath the starry sky to gaze at the stars
as you claim the wonders of the night sky as your own.
Know that in your quietude on the fallen snow
every single seed born of your asking has already germinated.

Bathe in deep waters to enjoy the rough seas
and wind chill as you ride out a storm.
You might even believe you will drown.
But you won't.
Instead the self pity will float away
and you will go back to the innocence of forgiveness.
You can always begin again with the breath.

Split life open to reveal that you long for a call from beyond.

Go ahead, search under every moss covered rock,

ponder every hawk in flight, ask every breeze that delights.

Don't forget to look to the ancient live oak for wisdom.

Most likely the answer will not arrive in the way you think it should.

It will come in the form of love,

as a formula for splendor;

an easy melody with Nature.

Trust the seed of this emerging promise.

Do not settle for less than the freedom and elegance

of mad wild enchantment with yourself amid the natural world.

From there you can take the joy you have gained

and open the hearts of all those you meet.

And I promise you, that you and I,

can change the world,

one precious breath at a time,

just you and I.

CPSIA information can be obtained
at www.ICGtesting.com
Printed in the USA
BVHW032033200221
600438BV00004B/11